A PICTURE BOOK OF
Daniel Boone

by David A. Adler *and* Michael S. Adler
illustrated by Matt Collins

Holiday House / New York

Daniel Boone stood on one of the Allegheny Mountains. He looked at the trees, flowers, and streams below. A huge herd of buffaloes ran through the valley. "An amazing country," he said. "Whoever beheld such abundance?"

It was 1769, and this was his first look at beautiful, unsettled Kentucky.

In the mid-1700s, when America was still ruled by England, Daniel Boone explored land beyond the borders of the thirteen American colonies. He later cleared a trail to Kentucky, the Wilderness Road, and people followed.

Daniel Boone was born on November 2, 1734, in a log cabin in Oley, in what is now Berks County, Pennsylvania, just north of Reading. He was the sixth of eleven children born to Squire and Sarah Boone.

The Boones were Quakers, who came to Pennsylvania from England seeking religious freedom. Squire Boone was a blacksmith, weaver, and farmer. He also kept a herd of cattle. He was a restless man, not happy in one place for long. His son Daniel would be restless too.

Daniel was a lively and curious child. He often forgot his chores and instead wandered in the nearby woods. When he was about twelve years old, his father gave him his first rifle. After that he often disappeared for a few days. When he returned, he had enough meat to feed his family for a week.

Squire's brother John was a schoolteacher. He complained that his nephew Daniel wasn't given a formal education. "Let the girls do the spelling," Squire Boone told his brother. "Dan will do the shooting, and between you and me that is what we most need."

In 1751, the Boones moved south. They settled in the Yadkin Valley of North Carolina, an area with lots of fish, wild turkeys, deer, and bears.

In the 1750s, England and France controlled much of the settled areas of North America. In 1754, the French and Indian War, a fight between France and Britain to control America, broke out. Native American tribes were divided, but mostly they sided with the French.

In June and July 1755, twenty-year-old Daniel Boone was a wagon driver in the service of Major General Edward Braddock, who led an attack against the French stronghold by the Ohio River. One of the approximately fifteen hundred British and colonial soldiers who marched with Braddock was Colonel George Washington.

The French and Native Americans hid in bushes and behind rocks and trees. Braddock's men stood in the open and were easy targets in their bright red uniforms. "They would fight," one British officer reported, "if they could see their enemy."

It was a terrible defeat for the British. Braddock was killed, and several hundred of his men were killed or wounded. During this disastrous expedition Daniel Boone heard a trader named John Findley talk of land west of the Allegheny Mountains, the western section of Virginia known as Kentucky. He said that a hunter could stand in one place and great herds of buffalo and deer would come to him. Those stories would change Boone's life.

After the battle, Boone returned home. Early in the summer of 1756, Boone went to a cherry-picking party. He sat in the grass with seventeen-year-old Rebecca Bryan, a tall, pretty woman with fair skin, dark hair, and dark eyes. She was strong and independent. Still, she was easygoing and kind. They married on August 14, 1756.

Rebecca and Daniel Boone had ten children. They also raised eight nieces and nephews. Their first home was on his father's land in what is now Davie County, North Carolina.

As a hunter, Daniel Boone was on a constant search for a better hunting ground. He was unable to stay in one place for very long. In 1765, he went with some friends on an expedition to Florida. Then, in late 1767, he set out to explore Kentucky.

His first expedition there was a failure. The rugged hills and winter weather forced him to turn back before reaching Kentucky.

On May 1, 1769, Boone set out again for Kentucky. Five other men went with him. They hunted and trapped animals. In December, Boone and his party were attacked by Shawnee Indians, who told them they were on Shawnee land. They took many of Boone's furs and supplies.

"We were often in a dangerous, helpless situation," Daniel Boone later said, "exposed daily to perils and death."

Four of the men left. They were on their way home when they met Daniel's brother Squire, who had come with supplies. They told him where to find Daniel. The two brothers stayed in Kentucky until May 1771.

Two years later, on September 25, 1773, Boone and his family and some fifty pioneers set off for Kentucky to establish a settlement there.

Soon after they arrived, Boone's eldest son, James, and several others were attacked and killed by a group of Shawnee Indians. Daniel Boone called the tragedy "the worst melancholy of my life."

Two years later, Boone and about thirty-five other pioneers cut a muddy path from northern Virginia through the Cumberland Gap along the Kentucky River to what is now Louisville, Kentucky. This route came to be called the Wilderness Trail. More settlers followed. They built a fort and named it Boonesborough in honor of Daniel Boone.

The coming of the Revolutionary War with Britain did little to slow frequent Shawnee attacks. "We are surrounded with enemies on every side," one settler said. "Every day increases their numbers."

In July 1776, the Shawnee captured Boone's fourteen-year-old daughter, Jemima, and two other girls. Boone and several other men followed a trail of cloth the girls had torn from their dresses. Boone found the girls, but the Shawnee captured him and tied him to a tree. Just before he was to be killed, Boone's men came to the rescue. Boone and the girls were saved.

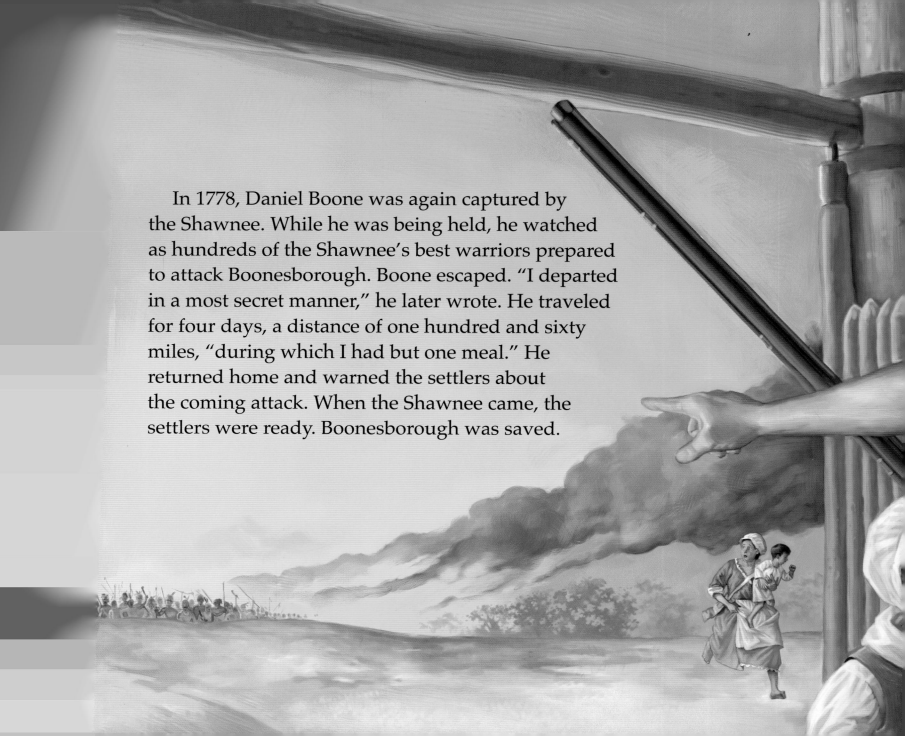

In 1778, Daniel Boone was again captured by the Shawnee. While he was being held, he watched as hundreds of the Shawnee's best warriors prepared to attack Boonesborough. Boone escaped. "I departed in a most secret manner," he later wrote. He traveled for four days, a distance of one hundred and sixty miles, "during which I had but one meal." He returned home and warned the settlers about the coming attack. When the Shawnee came, the settlers were ready. Boonesborough was saved.

In 1781, Kentucky was still part of the state of Virginia. That year Daniel Boone was elected to represent Kentucky in the Virginia General Assembly.

With the American victory in the Revolutionary War, Boone settled in what was later called Maysville, Kentucky. There he worked as a surveyor, horse trader, and land speculator.

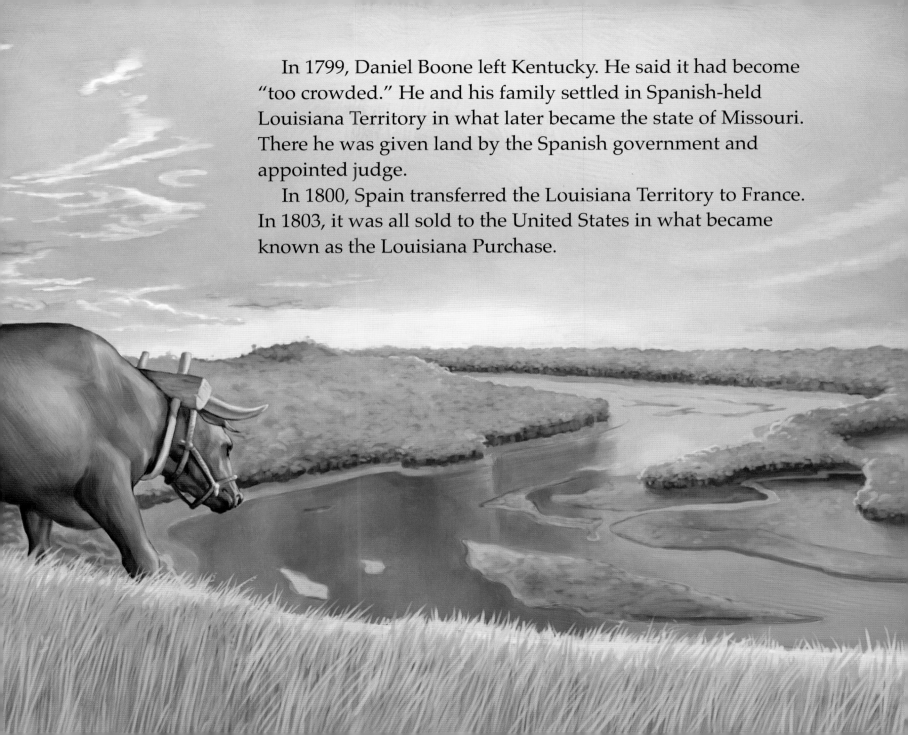

In 1799, Daniel Boone left Kentucky. He said it had become "too crowded." He and his family settled in Spanish-held Louisiana Territory in what later became the state of Missouri. There he was given land by the Spanish government and appointed judge.

In 1800, Spain transferred the Louisiana Territory to France. In 1803, it was all sold to the United States in what became known as the Louisiana Purchase.

Age eventually took its toll on Daniel Boone. He could no longer make long trips through the wilderness. He sang with his grandchildren and told them stories. He repaired rifles for his friends and neighbors.

On September 26, 1820, at the age of eighty-five, Daniel Boone died at his son's home in Missouri.

"Sometimes I feel like a leaf carried on a stream," Daniel Boone once wrote. "It may whirl and twist, but it is always carried forward." The leaf that was Daniel Boone had led Americans west.

IMPORTANT DATES

1734   Born in Oley, Pennsylvania, November 2.

1751   Boone family settles in Yadkin Valley, North Carolina.

1754–1755 Serves as a wagon driver for the British army in the French and Indian War.

1756   Marries Rebecca Bryan, August 14.

1760   After a nearby Cherokee Indian attack, the Boones move to Virginia.

1765   Explores Florida with several friends.

1767   Sets out to explore Kentucky in the fall before returning home because of rugged terrain.

1769   Sets out for Kentucky, May 1. His group is attacked by Shawnee Indians, December.

1773   Sets off for Kentucky, hoping to establish a colony there, September 25.

1775   Much of the Cherokee claim on Kentucky purchased by Richard Henderson, March.

1775   Builds Wilderness Road; Boonesborough established.

1776   Jemima Boone captured by Shawnee Indians.

1778   Surrenders to Shawnee after attack and is held captive for four months.

1781   Elected to represent Kentucky in the Virginia General Assembly.

1799   Leaves Kentucky for Missouri.

1813   Rebecca Boone dies.

1820   Dies in Missouri at his son Nathan's home, September 26.

SOURCE NOTES

Each source note includes the first word or words and the last word or words of a quotation and its source. References are to books cited in the Selected Bibliography.

"An amazing country . . . such abundance?": Boone, p. 46.

"Let the girls . . . what we most need.": Lofaro, p. 4.

"They would fight . . . see their enemy.": Irving, V1, p. 119.

"We were often . . . perils and death.": Boone, p. 4.

"the worst melancholy of my life,": Lawlor, p. 67.

"We are surrounded . . . increases their numbers.": Morgan, p. 217.

"I departed in . . . but one meal.": Boone, p. 14.

"too crowded.": Lofaro, p. 152.

"Sometimes I feel . . . carried forward.": Elliot, p. 74.

SELECTED BIBLIOGRAPHY

Boone, Daniel, and Francis Lister Hawks, *Daniel Boone's Own Story*. Mineola, New York: Dover, 2010.

Elliott, Lawrence. *The Long Hunter: A New Life of Daniel Boone*. New York: Reader's Digest Press, 1976.

Faragher, John Mack. *Daniel Boone: The Life and Legend of an American Pioneer*. New York: Henry Holt, 1992.

Lawlor, Laurie. *Daniel Boone*. Niles, Illinois: Whitman: 1989.

Lofaro, Michael A. *Daniel Boone: An American Life*. Lexington: The University Press of Kentucky, 2003.

Morgan, Robert. *Boone: A Biography*. Chapel Hill, North Carolina: Algonquin, 2007.

WEBSITES

www.danielboonehomestead.org/history.html

http://library.thinkquest.org/4034/daniel_boone.html

www.danielboonetrail.com

AUTHORS' NOTES

In 1734, when Daniel Boone was born, his birth date was said to be October 22. In 1752, the Gregorian calendar was adopted, and eleven days were added to the calendar. Boone's birth date became November 2.

Though mostly concerned with survival in the wilderness, the Boonesborough colonists were patriotic and supportive of the American colonists' battle for independence. In June 1776, Boonesborough residents wrote to the Virginia government that they would help the cause of American freedom in any way they could.

There is dispute as to where Daniel and Rebecca are now buried. In 1845, their remains were believed to have been exhumed and moved to Kentucky. Missourians, perhaps angered at the reburial, long claimed that the wrong bodies had been dug up.

To my nieces Aviva and Sara
and to their wonderful parents
—M. S. A.

To my grandfather G. P. Overmyer
—M. C.

Text copyright © 2013 by David A. Adler and Michael S. Adler
Illustrations copyright © 2013 by Matt Collins
All Rights Reserved
HOLIDAY HOUSE is registered in the U.S. Patent and Trademark Office.
Printed and Bound in April 2013 at Toppan Leefung, DongGuan City, China.
The text typeface is Palatino.
The artwork was created in Corel Painter.
www.holidayhouse.com
First Edition
1 3 5 7 9 10 8 6 4 2

Library of Congress Cataloging-in-Publication Data
Adler, David A.
A picture book of Daniel Boone / by David A. Adler and Michael S. Adler ; illustrated by Matt Collins.
p. cm.
Audience: Ages 4-8.
ISBN 978-0-8234-2748-2 (hbk.)
1. Boone, Daniel, 1734-1820—Juvenile literature. 2. Kentucky—Biography—Juvenile literature. 3. Pioneers—Kentucky—Biography—Juvenile literature.
4. Explorers—Kentucky—Biography—Juvenile literature. 5. Frontier and pioneer life—Kentucky—Juvenile literature.
6. Kentucky—Discovery and exploration—Juvenile literature. I. Adler, Michael S. II. Collins, Matt, ill. III. Title.
F454.B66A37 2013
976.9'02092—dc23
[B]
2012015945